INDIAN
VEGETARIAN COOKING

INDIAN RECIPES FOR
THE ADVENTUROUS COOK

INDIAN
VEGETARIAN COOKING

INDIAN RECIPES FOR
THE ADVENTUROUS COOK

Quantum
Books

A QUANTUM BOOK

Published by
Quantum Books Ltd
6 Blundell Street
London N7 9BH

1-86160-200-6

Project Manager: Rebecca Kingsley
Designer: Bruce Low
Editor: Sarah Harris

The material in this publication previously appeared in
Step-by-Step Indian Cooking
The Hot and Spicy Cookbook

QUMVGID
Set in Fritz Quadrata
Reproduced in Singapore by Eray Scan
Printed in Singapore by Star Standard Industries (Pte) Ltd

Contents

INTRODUCTION

The continent of India is home to some of the most varied and popular dishes in the world. The vast selection of herbs and spices that grow in each region provide a wealth of tastes and flavours from the mild and subtle to the hot and fiery. Although many dishes include rich, creamy sauces, the sheer variety of ingredients mean that Indian food includes a wide range of nutritional recipes.

Indian cookery also offers diversity to those looking for a meat-free diet, as many Indian dishes are vegetable-based, or can be easily adapted to suit a vegetarian diet. Indeed, vegetarianism has a religious basis throughout India. Although Muslims may eat meat - except pork - and some other sects forbid the killing of certain animals, other Indian religions, such as the Hindu and Jain faiths, demand a meat-free diet.

Religious and moral beliefs also account for many people turning to vegetarianism in the West, although often the choice of a meat-free diet is a decision based on health reasons. Indian vegetarian cookery represents an ideal choice for anyone looking to maintain a healthy diet, being generally low in fat, and containing a variety of nutritional herbs and spices.

It is the use of herbs and spices that gives Indian cookery its reputation for diverse tastes and flavours. With around 25 spices to choose from, it is no wonder that generations of cooks have been able to create an almost infinite variety of recipes. Often the choice of spices and herbs was not solely dependent on their taste, but

also on their medicinal qualities, meaning that in Indian cookery, nutrition and flavour go hand in hand. Most of these spices are readily available in supermarkets, whether in fresh or dried form.

Even given the West's familiarity with Indian cuisine today, there is still a common misconception that Indian food is very hot. While some dishes do have a particularly potent blend of spices, there is a considerable amount of subtlety in Indian cookery. Some of this diversity comes from the range of temperature extremes to be found in India. Some parts of India suffer from severe cold during parts of the

year. A dish flavoured with warming spices would certainly be an effective measure against the biting cold. By contrast, a dish prepared using mild spices can help to offset the harsh, dry heat that is prevalent in other parts of the continent.

As well as adapting the use of herbs and spices according to temperature, Indian dishes also differ on a regional level, according to the availability of local produce and traditional cooking methods. A general look at this division, for example, shows that breads tend to be eaten in the north of India, while rice is more common in the south. A similar difference is apparent in the common methods of cooking. In the north most meals are cooked in an oven, while those in the south favour steaming.

In the West, the traditional way to serve meal is in courses - starter, main course and dessert. By contrast, Indian food is generally made up of several dishes, which are traditionally served together - savoury and sweet dishes alike. Cutlery is not traditionally used. Food is scooped up with flat breads or mopped up with rice and eaten with the hands. However, it is the right hand only which touches the food, as the left hand is considered unclean. How much of the hand is used depends on the part of India the dish is served in. Some areas favour the use of just the fingertips, others utilise the whole hand.

Although traditional preparation methods are still employed in parts of India, modern equipment is often a simpler option. While a mortar and pestle is useful when grinding small quantities of spices or seeds, a coffee grinder or blender is quicker and easier when mixing larger quantities.

In much of Indian cookery, the even distribution of heat when cooking is essential. As the old-fashioned method of cooking in a charcoal fire is not practical in our western kitchens, a good set of cast-iron saucepans and casseroles is the best modern alternative. Cast iron pans both transmit and hold the heat well. Food also tends to stick to cast iron less than to enamel.

Most of the other equipment required for Indian cooking can generally be found in a well-stocked kitchen anyway. This equipment includes sharp knives, a colander, grater, wooden spoons and skewers.

Indian vegetarian cookery represents the perfect choice for anyone looking to experiment with herbs and spices, while maintaining a healthy, nutritionally

balanced diet. The proliferation of fresh fruits and vegetables today means that you are almost spoilt for choice when choosing ingredients for your meal.

The recipes in this book have been specially chosen to provide a diverse range of flavours and textures to suit all palates. From the hot and spicy to the creamy and mild, from the sweet to the savoury, these recipes will enable the adventurous cook to create a selection of menus that will appeal to all tastes.

Chapter One

Chutneys and Snacks

Tamarind Chutney

■

Black Lentil Chutney

■

Yogurt and Tomato Relish

■

Green Corriander Chutney

TAMARIND CHUTNEY

Amli Chatni

INGREDIENTS

50g (2 oz) Juice from seedless tamarind
1 tbsp coriander seeds
1 tsp peppercorns
½ tsp cumin seeds
½ tsp fenugreek seeds
1 tsp mustard seeds
½ tsp asafoetida
5 red chillies
2–3 tbsp oil
1 tsp polished split black lentils (urid dal)
1 tsp chana dal soaked for 20 minutes, then drained
6 curry leaves
1 oz shelled peanuts
2 tbsp brown sugar
Salt
1 tbsp sesame seeds
25-50g (1–2 oz) desiccated coconut

Heat a frying pan without any butter or oil and add the coriander, peppercorns, cumin, fenugreek, half the mustard seeds, half the asafoetida and 4 red chillies. Roast the spices for about 5 minutes. shaking the pan to prevent burning; pound or grind the spices to a fine powder and set aside.

Heat the oil in a pan, add the remaining mustard seeds, the dal, lentils, curry leaves and remaining chilli, cut into 3 or 4 pieces, and fry until all the seeds have popped.

Add the peanuts and fry for a further 3 or 4 minutes, then add the tamarind juice, the roasted spice powder, sugar, ½ tsp salt and remaining asafoetida.

Heat another pan without fat or oil, roast the sesame seeds and coconut and add to the chutney. Stir well, adding extra salt to taste.

BLACK LENTIL CHUTNEY
Urid Dal Chatni

Pick over the dal. Heat a pan without fat or oil, add the dal, 1 chilli and the asafoetida and cook, shaking the pan to prevent burning, until the dal is golden.

Pound the roasted spices together.

Grind, pound or blend in a liquidizer the coconut and tamarind with 1–2 tablespoons water, then add the roasted spice powder and grind them together, adding a little more if necessary.

Add salt to taste.

INGREDIENTS

75-100g (3–4 oz) polished split black lentils (urid dal)
1 or 2 red chillies
¼ tsp asafoetida
50g (2 oz) finely grated coconut
Juice from 25g (1 oz) seedless tamarind (see below)
Salt

SQUEEZING TAMARINDS

Break of 50g (2oz) tamarind from the block and soak it in twice its volume of very hot water for a couple of hours. Now squeeze the pulp well or press it through a sieve with a wooden spoon to get out all the juice.

YOGURT AND TOMATO RELISH

Tamatar Raita

INGREDIENTS

125g (5 oz) yogurt

25g (10 oz) tomatoes, diced

1 small onion, finely chopped leaves from

1 sprig of coriander

1 green chilli, finely chopped12g (½ oz) fresh ginger, finely grated

½ tsp salt

Mix the tomato with the onion. You can reduce the strength of the onion by rinsing it in hot water, if preferred.

Mix the yogurt with the remaining ingredients. Stir the dressing into the vegetables and add extra salt to taste.

Green Coriander Chutney

Hari Daniya Chatni

Ingredients

Leaves from 3–4 sprigs coriander
1 or 2 green chillies
12g (½ oz) fresh ginger, grated
Salt
2 tbsp lemon juice
½ tsp sugar

Grind, pound or blend in a liquidizer the coriander leaves, green chilli, ginger and ½ tsp salt to make a thick paste.

Stir in the lemon juice and add sugar and extra salt to taste.

Chapter Two

Main Courses

Onion Bhajis

■

Melon with Curry Mayonnaise

■

Curried Parsnip Soup

■

Vegetable Curry

■

Saffron Rice and Almond Salad

■

Ripe Mango Curry

■

Buttermilk Curry

■

Green Beans and Potato Torran

■

Vegetable Biriyani

■

Mashed Aubergine

■

Stuffed Okra

■

Spinach Torran

■

Cauliflower with Potato and Tomatoes

■

Green Papaya Torran

■

Stuffed Bitter Gourds

■

Red Peppers stuffed with Vegetables

Onion Bhajis

MAKES 10–12

Heat the oil and fry the spices for a minute. Add the onion, and stir until well coated.

Turn down the heat, cover, and cook until the onion is tender but not mushy. Leave to cool.

Add salt, egg and gram (chick pea) flour and stir well.

Fry generous half-tablespoonfuls of the mixture in 1½ cm hot oil, turning them almost immediately. As soon as they are puffy and brown remove them with a slotted spoon and drain on kitchen paper . Serve warm.

Onion Bhajis can be kept warm in a moderate oven for 20 minutes or so before serving, but they cannot be made in advance and reheated.

Variation

Make the bhajis half-size and serve with toothpicks or cocktail sticks.

Ingredients

2 tbsp oil
½ tsp ground mustard seed
1 tsp fenugreek seed
1 tsp ground turmeric
1 medium onion, finely chopped
Pinch chilli powder (optional)
½ tsp salt
1 egg
50g (2 oz) gram (chick pea) flour
Oil for frying

INGREDIENTS

2 ripe, pink-flesh melons about 300g (12 oz) each
Approx. 25g (1 oz) mayonnaise
1–2 tbsp singlecream
Curry paste to taste
A little lime or lemon juice

MELON WITH CURRY MAYONNAISE

SERVES 4

Halve the melons and scrape out the seeds. Either scoop out most of the flesh with a melon baller, or use a spoon and cut the flesh into bite-sized chunks. Turn the shells upside down to drain.

Mix the mayonnaise with the cream (you might need more cream if the mayonnaise is very thick and home-made) and add curry paste and lime or lemon juice to taste. The dressings should be delicate.

Combine the melon flesh with the dressing, pile back into the shells and chill before serving.

Ingredients

Generous 500g (1 lb) parsnips
4 tbsp butter
1½ tsp ground coriander
1 tsp ground cumin
½ tsp ground turmeric
Approx. 750ml (25 floz) milk and stock or water, mixed
Few drops Tabasco
Salt and white pepper to taste
2 tbsp single cream
Chopped fresh coriander or parsley

Curried Parsnip Soup

SERVES 3–4

Scrub and trim the parsnips and chop into 2 cm dice. Cover with cold water until needed.

Melt the butter in a heavy saucepan and fry the spices in it without browning to release the flavours.

Add the drained parsnips and turn until well coated. Add the milk and stock or water and simmer, covered, for 20 minutes or so, until the parsnips are just tender.

Sieve, liquidize or process the soup; it should not be absolutely smooth.

Reheat and season to taste with Tabasco, salt and white pepper.

Serve with a swirl of cream in each bowl, together with a sprinkling of fresh coriander or parsley.

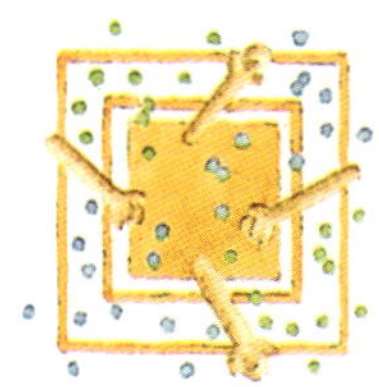

VEGETABLE CURRY

SERVES 4–6

INGREDIENTS

1–2 fresh green chillies, seeded and chopped
2 cloves garlic, minced
2 tbsp ghee or oil
1 tsp ground turmeric
1 tbsp Garam Masala
1 tsp mustard seed, crushed
1 tsp ground coriander
2 tbsp lime or lemon juice
2 medium onions, chopped
1 large potato, peeled and cubed
450g (1 lb) mixed prepared vegetables, such as: caulifloweretts; string or snap beans, stringed and sliced; shelled peas; washed spinach, tough stems removed; etc.
2 ripe tomatoes, peeled and chopped
Approx. 8 fl oz water
Salt, pepper and sugar to taste

Fry the chillies and garlic in the ghee or oil with the spices, and lime or lemon juice for 5 minutes.

Add the onion, and stir over a high heat until it begins to brown.

Add the vegetables, water and seasoning and simmer, uncovered and stirring occasionally, until the potato is cooked and most of the liquid evaporated—about 20 minutes. Serve hot.

INGREDIENTS

200g (8 oz) long-grain rice
600ml (1 pt) water
Good pinch salt
½ tsp saffron threads infused for ½ hour in
2 tbsp hot water
½ tsp English mustard
1 tbsp wine vinegar
3 tbsp olive oil
1 tsp sugar
75-100g (3–4 oz) blanched almonds
1–2 fresh chillies, seeded, rinsed and thinly sliced (optional)

SAFFRON RICE AND ALMOND SALAD

SERVES 6

Put the rice, water, salt and saffron infusion in a saucepan, bring to a boil and simmer, covered, until the water has been absorbed and the rice is just tender, about 20 to 25 minutes. Take off the heat.

Combine the mustard, vinegar, oil and sugar and stir into the hot rice. Chill.

Just before serving, toast the almonds under the broiler or in a moderate oven, shaking the pan from time to time, until lightly browned. Stir into the chilled rice with the chillies, if used, and serve immediately. (If this salad is kept sitting around the almonds will lose their crunch.)

INGREDIENTS

4 small sweet ripe mangoes, cubed, with the skin left on
2 tsp chilli powder
½ tsp turmeric
Salt
Grated flesh of ½ coconut
½ tsp ground cumin
6 curry leaves
2 tbsp oil
2 tsp mustard seeds
2 tsp fenugreek seeds
2 red chillies, cut into 4 pieces
2–3 tsp sugar

RIPE MANGO CURRY

Aam Curry

SERVES 4

Cook the mango in about 600ml (1 pt) water with the chilli powder, turmeric and 1 teaspoon salt, for about 5 minutes, making sure that the mango does not lose its shape.

Blend the coconut with the cumin and add to the mango with half the curry leaves.

Heat the oil in a frying pan and when hot, add the mustard seeds. Let them sizzle for a few seconds until they have all popped, then add the fenugreek seeds, red chilli and remaining curry leaves. Stir and fry for a few seconds, then add to the mango. Stir well and add sugar and salt to taste.

BUTTERMILK CURRY

Morkari

SERVES 4

INGREDIENTS

600 ml (1 pt) soured buttermilk, made by stirring
300ml (2 tbsp) water into 1 cup yogurt
50g (2 oz) red pumpkin, peeled and cubed
50g (2 oz) potatoes, peeled and cubed
1 hard green banana, peeled and thickly sliced
½ tsp turmeric
½ tsp chilli powder
2 tsp salt
Grated flesh of ½ coconut
½ tsp ground cumin
2 tbsp oil
1 tsp mustard seeds
½ tsp fenugreek seeds
1 or 2 red chillies, cut into 3 or 4 pieces
6–8 curry leaves

Simmer the pumpkin, potato and banana in a pan of water with the turmeric, chilli powder and 1 teaspoon salt for 10–15 minutes, until cooked. Drain and keep hot.

In a bowl, blend the coconut with the cumin, then stir in the buttermilk.

Stir the buttermilk mixture into the vegetables over a low heat. Cook for 3–4 minutes, until hot through, stirring all the time, so that the buttermilk does not separate. Set aside, covered.

Heat the oil in a frying pan and add the mustard seeds, fenugreek seeds and red chilli. Let them sizzle for a few seconds until all the mustard seeds have popped. Add to the curry.

Add salt to taste and sprinkle on the curry leaves.

Green Beans and Potato Toran

Aloo Hari Moong Toran

SERVES 2

Ingredients

50g (2 oz) green beans, trimmed and cut into 2½ cm lengths
50g (2 oz) potatoes, peeled and diced
75-100g (2–3 oz) butter or ghee
1 small onion, finely chopped
50g (2 oz) tomatoes, peeled and finely chopped
½ tsp garam masala
½ tsp turmeric
½ tsp chilli powder
1 green chilli, cut into pieces
12g (½ oz) fresh ginger, finely grated
1 clove garlic, finely chopped
Leaves from 1 sprig of coriander
Salt

Heat the butter or ghee in a large saucepan and fry the onion until golden.

Add the tomato, stir well and squash it with the back of a wooden spoon until it forms a paste.

Add the garam masala, turmeric and chilli powder and continue to fry, stirring for about 5 minutes.

Add the beans, potatoes, green chilli, ginger, garlic and coriander leaves with 1 tablespoon water and cook gently over a low heat, with the lid tightly on, stirring occasionally, for 10–15 minutes, until the vegetables are done. Add salt to taste.

VEGETABLE BIRIYANI

Sabzi Biriyani

SERVES 4–6

Grind or pound the fennel seeds, turmeric, cardamom seeds, cinnamon, cloves and poppy seeds. Blend in a liquidizer with the garlic, ginger, green chilli and coriander leaves.

Heat the butter or ghee in a pan, add half the onion and fry until golden.

Add the blended spices, the bay leaves and tomato and continue to cook, mashing the tomato under the back of a wooden spoon to make a thick paste.

Pour on 300ml (½ pt) water, add the carrots, potatoes, peas and ½ tsp salt and bring to a boil. Simmer for about 15 minutes, until the potatoes are cooked, and the sauce is thick.

Meanwhile, prepare the rice. Pick over the rice, wash in 2 or 3 changes of water, then soak for 15–20 minutes. Drain thoroughly.

Heat the butter or ghee in a pan, add the onion and crumble over the bay leaf. Fry until the onion is golden.

Pour on enough boiling water to cover the rice and cook, covered, for 10 minutes. Then turn off the heat and leave, covered, for 5–10 minutes until the liquid is absorbed and the rice is tender but not soft.

Stir the vegetables into the rice and heat through. Add extra salt to taste.

Fry the cashew nuts briefly in ghee and sprinkle over the curry.

INGREDIENTS

50g (2 oz) tomatoes, peeled and chopped
25g (1 oz) carrots, peeled and diced
50g (2 oz) potatoes, peeled and diced
25g (1 oz) fresh peas
½ tsp fennel seeds
½ tsp turmeric
Cardamom seeds from 1 pod
2½ cm cinnamon stick
3 cloves
1 tsp poppy seeds
2 cloves garlic, chopped
12g (½ oz) fresh ginger, grated
2 green chillies, chopped
Leaves from 1 sprig of coriander
50g (2 oz) butter or ghee
1 small onion, chopped
2 bay leaves
Salt

For the rice

275-360g (10–12 oz) basmati rice
50g (2 oz) butter or ghee
1 onion, finely chopped
1 bay leaf
About 50g (2 oz) cashew nuts
50g (2 oz) ghee

MASHED AUBERGINE

Baigan Bharta

SERVES 2

Put the aubergine in a roasting tin and cook in the oven at 200°C/400°F/gas6 for 40 minutes or until the inside is cooked. Allow the aubergine to cool, then peel off the skin and immerse the vegetable in cold water.

Heat the butter or ghee in a pan and add the onion, half the coriander leaves, the garlic, ginger, garam masala, green chilli, turmeric, cumin and chilli powder. Stir and fry until the onion is golden.

Meanwhile, drain the aubergine and mash with a fork.

When the butter runs out of the spice paste, add the aubergine and ½ tsp salt, stir thoroughly and cook for 3–4 minutes to heat through.

Sprinkle on the remaining coriander leaves and the lemon juice. Add more salt to taste if liked.

INGREDIENTS

1 aubergine
50-75g (2–3 oz) butter or ghee
1 onion, finely chopped
Leaves from 1 sprig of coriander
1 clove garlic, chopped
12g (½ oz) fresh ginger, finely grated
½ tsp garam masala
1 green chilli, sliced
½ tsp turmeric
½ tsp cumin
½ tsp chilli powder
50g (2 oz) tomatoes, peeled and chopped
Salt
1 tbsp lemon juice

STUFFED OKRA

Sabu Bhindi

SERVES 2

Wash the okra and dry on paper towels. Cut off the stalks and slice the okra in half lengthways.

Mix together the spices and salt.

Stuff the okra with the spice mix and leave them to stand in a cool place for at least 30 minutes.

Heat the oil and fry the okra for about 4 minutes, turning carefully, to cook on all sides.

INGREDIENTS

1 cup okra

½ tsp paprika

½ tsp chili powder

1 tbsp mango powder (amchur)

½ tsp ground ginger

Salt

4 tbsp oil

SPINACH TORAN

Palak Toran

SERVES 2

Wash the spinach, discard any discoloured leaves and tough stalks, and shake dry. Chop as finely as possible and leave in a colander to drain.

Heat the oil in a pan and gently fry the onion and green chilli until the onion is transparent.

Add the spinach and tomato, cover tightly and cook on a low heat for 4–5 minutes, shaking the pan occasionally, until the spinach has collapsed.

Stir in the coconut and add salt to taste.

INGREDIENTS

450g (1 lb) fresh spinach
4 tbsp oil
1 small onion, finely chopped
1 green chilli, chopped
75g (3 oz) tomatoes, peeled and chopped
75g (3 oz) grated or desiccated coconut
Salt

CAULIFLOWER WITH POTATO AND TOMATOES

Aloo Gobi Tamatar Masala

SERVES 4

Peel the potato and cut into chunks. Divide the cauliflower into florets, discarding the tough stalks. Put the vegetables in a pan of cold water to prevent discoloration.

Heat three-quarters of the butter or ghee in a heavy-bottomed pan and add the onion, ginger, garlic, green chilli and half the coriander leaves. Stir and fry until the onion is golden.

Stir in the tomato, add the chili powder, turmeric, coriander, fennel seeds, garam masala and half the cumin and cook over a low heat, squashing the tomato under the back of a wooden spoon to make a thick paste.

Drain and add the vegetables with about 4 tablespoon water. Cover and cook, stirring occasionally, for about 15 minutes, until the potato is tender but not soft.

Meanwhile, heat the remaining butter or ghee in a separate pan and when hot, add the remaining ground cumin. Add to the curry with the remaining coriander leaves and salt to taste.

INGREDIENTS

450g (1 lb) cauliflower
75g (3 oz) potato
50g (2 oz) butter or ghee
1 small onion, finely chopped
12g (½ oz) fresh ginger, finely grated
1 clove garlic, finely chopped
2 green chillies, cut into 4–6 pieces
Leaves from 1 sprig of coriander
25g (1 oz) tomatoes, peeled and roughly chopped
½ tsp chilli powder
½ tsp turmeric
½ tsp ground coriander
½ tsp fennel seeds
½ tsp ground cumin
Salt

GREEN PAPAYA TORAN

Papaya Toran

SERVES 2

Cook the papaya in salted water to cover for 10–15 minutes, until tender but not soft. Drain and keep hot.

Heat the oil in a frying pan and add the dal, onion, mustard seeds, curry leaves and red chilli. Fry until the onion is golden, then add the papaya, stir and fry for 3–4 minutes.

Stir in the grated coconut and add salt to taste.

INGREDIENTS

450g (1 lb) unripe green papaya, peeled and cubed

Salt

2 tbsp oil

2 tsp polished split black lentils (urid dal)

1 small onion, finely chopped

1 tsp mustard seeds

4–6 curry leaves

1 red chilli, cut into 4 or 6 pieces

25g (1 oz) grated or desiccated coconut

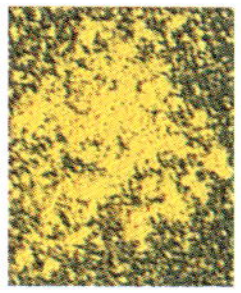

STUFFED BITTER GOURDS

Sabu Karela

SERVES 4

Scrape the gourds and slit them lengthways from the tip, leaving the 2 halves joined at the stalk. Sprinkle salt both inside and out and leave the gourds in a cool place for 15 minutes.

Scrape away the seeds and squeeze the gourds to remove the moisture drawn from them by the salt.

Mix together the chilli powder, mango powder and remaining salt.

Sprinkle the insides of the gourds with oil and stuff the spice mixture well down inside them. Tie the gourds together with thread.

Heat the remaining oil over a low heat and fry the gourds, turning gently for 5–10 minutes, until cooked. Remove thread.

Serve hot or cold.

INGREDIENTS

450g (1 lb) bitter gourds

1 tsp salt

1 tsp chilli powder

2 tbsp mango powder (amchur)

4 tbsp oil

RED PEPPERS STUFFED WITH VEGETABLES

Lal Mirchi Sabzi

SERVES 4

Peel the potatoes, dice them and leave in a pan of cold water to prevent discolouration.

Heat the butter or ghee in a pan, add the onion, ginger and garlic and fry until the onion is golden.

Add the tomato, turmeric, chilli powder, ½ teaspoon salt and ground coriander, cook and stir briskly, squashing the tomato under the back of a wooden spoon to make a thick paste.

Drain the potato and add to the spice mix with 2–4 tablespoon water. Cover and cook on a low heat, stirring occasionally, for 10–15 minutes, until the potato is tender but not soft.

Add the garam masala and coriander leaves. Cook for a further 3–4 minutes, then set aside, covered.

Wash the peppers and with a sharp knife, cut off the top, which can be used as a lid. Scrape them out and discard the seeds and pith.

Stuff the peppers with the potato curry and replace the lids.

Heat the oil in a pan, put in the peppers and fry gently on all sides until cooked, about 15 minutes. Alternatively, stand the peppers in a greased dish, cover and cook in the oven at 200°C/400°F/gas 6 for 30 minutes, until tender.

INGREDIENTS

4 large red peppers
150g (6 oz) potatoes
50-75 (2–3 oz) butter or ghee
1 small onion, finely chopped
½ oz fresh ginger, finely grated
1 clove garlic, finely chopped
25g (1 oz) tomatoes, peeled and chopped
½ tsp turmeric
½ tsp chilli powder
Salt
½ tsp ground coriander
½ tsp garam masala
Leaves from 1 sprig of coriander
2 tbsp oil

Chapter Four

Desserts

Cardamom Crumble with Apricots

■

Creole Bananas

■

Birthday Bread-and-Butter Pudding

■

Pumpkin Halva

■

Cinnamon Toast Ice-Cream

■

Mango Souffle

■

Pineapple Pudding

■

Old-Fashioned Rice Pudding

■

Plantain Jaggery

CARDAMOM CRUMBLE WITH APRICOTS

SERVES 4–6

Put the apricots and 6 or 7 of the cardamom pods in a saucepan and pour over them the boiling water. Cover and leave to soak for a couple of hours, or overnight, then simmer gently until the apricots are soft—between 25 and 45 minutes, depending on how dry the apricots were and how long they were soaked. Leave to cool.

Remove the black seeds from the remaining cardamom pods and grind them with the white sugar in a spice or coffee grinder or pepper mill. Reserve.

For the crumble topping, rub into the butter the flour, light brown sugar and half the ground cardamom mixture until the mixture resembles coarse crumbs. Chill until needed.

To assemble, discard the cooked pods and mash the apricots to a coarse purée. Add lemon juice to taste. Spread over the bottom of a lightly greased gratin dish or four individual ramekin dishes. The purée should be no more than ¾ inch thick. Sprinkle the surface with the remaining ground cardamom mixture and top with the crumble.

Bake in a preheated oven for 20 to 30 minutes, until the crumble topping is crisp and pale gold. Serve warm with lots of single cream.

INGREDIENTS

50g (2 oz) dried apricots
8–9 cardamom pods
Approx. 375ml (12½ Floz) boiling water
1 tsp white sugar
12g (½ oz) butter, diced
25 g (1 oz) plain flour, sifted
12g (½ oz) light brown sugar
A little lemon juice

OVEN TEMPERATURE:
200°C/400°F/GAS6

INGREDIENTS

6 medium bananas, ripe
3 tbsp butter
12g (½ oz) light brown sugar
12g (½ oz) dark rum
Approx. 1 tbsp lime or lemon juice
Freshly grated nutmeg

OVEN TEMPERATURE:
180°C/350°F/GAS4

CREOLE BANANAS

SERVES 4

Peel the bananas, halve them lengthwise and arrange them in a single layer in a large baking dish. Dot with the butter, sprinkle on the sugar and add the rum and lime or lemon juice, more if it seems too sweet.

Dust the bananas with a light grating of nutmeg and bake in a preheated oven for 35 to 40 minutes, until the bananas are tender, brown and aromatic.

Serve hot or warm with plenty of singlecream.

BIRTHDAY BREAD-AND-BUTTER PUDDING

SERVES 4

INGREDIENTS

4 thin slices buttered bread, crusts removed, cut in half
50g (2 oz) chopped candied citrus peel
50-75g (2–3 oz) blanched pistachios, halved
50g (2 oz) muscatel raisins, halved
450 ml (15 fl oz) single cream
4–5 cardamom pods
25g (1 oz) sugar
3 egg yolks, lightly beaten

OVEN TEMPERATURE:
180°C/350°F/GAS4

Layer the bread slices in a greased ovenproof dish with the peel, pistachios and raisins, if used.

Heat the cream with the cardamoms and sugar until almost boiling and pour onto the egg yolks, stirring well.

Strain the mixture over the bread, adding the cardamoms if you would like a stronger flavour.

Set the dish in a roasting pan half-full of hot water and bake until the crust has browned and the custard set, about 30 minutes. Serve warm.

PUMPKIN HALVA

Pethi Halva

SERVES 4

INGREDIENTS

450g (1 lb) pumpkin (preferably white)
600ml (1 pt) milk
125g (5 oz) sugar
1 tsp rose water
100g (4 oz) ghee
¼ tsp ground cardamom seeds
10–15 cashew nuts, halved

Scrape the seeds and stringy bits from the inside of the pumpkin, cut the flesh from the skin and chop into chunks.

Grate the pumpkin coarsely, put in a muslin cloth and squeeze out all the moisture.

Put the pumpkin in a pan with the milk, sugar and rose water and cook over a low heat for 30 minutes or more, stirring briskly, until all the milk has evaporated.

Stir in the ghee and continue cooking until it separates. Drain off any butter not absorbed by the pumpkin mixture.

Stir in the cardamom and cashew nuts and spread the mixture in a greased dish with straight sides, in one layer about 5 cm deep.

Leave for about 45 minutes, until set, then cut into squares.

Cinnamon Toast Ice Cream

SERVES 4–6

Mix the bread crumbs, brown sugar and cinnamon and bake for 20 to 25 minutes, until crisp and browned. As the crumbs will not brown evenly, take them out from time to time and fork those at the edges of the pan to the middle.

Leave the cooked crumbs to cool in the pan, then either grind or pound them coarsely and store in an airtight container until needed.

To make the ice cream, dissolve the white sugar in the water over a low heat until the bottom of the pan no longer feels "gritty" when tapped with a wooden spoon.

Turn up the heat and boil until a little of the syrup will draw out to a short thread between your forefinger and thumb. Take the pan off the heat and leave to stand for 30 seconds.

Pour the hot sugar syrup onto the egg yolks, whisking all the while, and continue to whisk over cold water or ice cubes until the mixture pales, thickens and cools. Add the vanilla extract.

Whip the chilled cream to soft peaks and stir it into the egg mixture.

Freeze the ice cream in a metal container, stirring from time to time to break down the ice crystals. When half frozen, beat it—easiest in an electric mixer—until smooth. Stir in most of the cinnamon crumbs. Pack and freeze until firm.

Transfer the ice cream to the refrigerator half an hour before serving. Sprinkle each bowlful with the remaining crumbs.

Ingredients

50g (2 oz) brown bread crumbs
35g (1½ oz) brown sugar
35g (1½ oz) ground cinnamon
65g (2½ oz) white sugar
½ cup water
3 egg yolks, lightly beaten
1 tsp vanilla extract
Scant 600ml (1 pt) chilled cream

OVEN TEMPERATURE:
200°F/400°F/GAS6

MANGO SOUFFLE

Aam Pudding

SERVES 4

Separate the eggs, putting the yolks into a mixing bowl.

In a small bowl, mix the gelatin with 3 tablespoons water.

Beat the yolks well and mix thoroughly with the mango juice or pulp.

Stir in the granulated sugar, gelatin and ½ teaspoon salt.

Put the mixing bowl over a pan of boiling water, taking care that the bowl does not touch the water or the eggs will scramble. Beat the mixture for 10 minutes, then take off the heat.

Whisk the egg whites with ½ teaspoon salt and castor sugar until stiff, then fold into the yolks, adding the vanilla flavouring.

Divide the mixture between 4 small dishes and chill before serving.

INGREDIENTS

300ml (½ pt) mango juice or 50g (2 oz) mango pulp
4 eggs
2 tsp gelatin
2 tbsp granulated sugar
Salt
2 tbsp castor sugar
½ tsp vanilla flavouring

INGREDIENTS

50g (2 oz)1 cup canned pineapple chunks, drained
2 eggs
150ml (¼ pt) milk
100g (4 oz) sugar
¼ tsp ground cinnamon
3 cloves

PINEAPPLE PUDDING

Ananas Pudding

SERVES 2

Arrange the pineapple pieces in a greased ovenproof dish.

Beat the eggs with the milk and sugar and pour over the pineapple, then sprinkle on the cinnamon and cloves.

Set the dish in a roasting tray of boiling water and cook in the oven at 165°C/325°F/gas3 for about 45 minutes until lightly set.

OLD-FASHIONED RICE PUDDING

SERVES 6–8

Grease an ovenproof dish with the butter and add the rest of the ingredients, except for the nutmeg.

Stir lightly and bake for about 3 hours.

Sprinkle with nutmeg and serve warm, with cream.

INGREDIENTS

Knob of butter
65g (2½ oz) pudding rice
1500 ml (2½ pt) creamy milk
12g (½ oz) sugar
Vanilla pod or 12g (½ oz) vanilla sugar
50g (2 oz) raisins, preferably muscatel
50g (2 oz) almonds, blanched and split
Freshly grated nutmeg

OVEN TEMPERATURE:
150°C/300°F/GAS2

PLANTAIN JAGGERY

Kela Gur

SERVES 4

INGREDIENTS

4 ripe plantain, unpeeled
150g (6 oz) jaggery; (raw sugar; use brown sugar if jaggery is not available)

Cut the plantain into 5 cm lengths, put in a pan and add just enough water to cover.

Add the jaggery and cook for 35–40 minutes, until all the water has evaporated.

Allow to cool, peel, then chill and serve cold.